SKILLS FOCUS

Promoting

f at

iew

n Miller

TROTMAN

About the author

Ron Miller is a science graduate who has worked in industry and been a management consultant and training advisor. Currently he runs a telecoms business and is a JP. He has written two books and various items for periodicals.

This first edition published in 1998 by Trotman and Company Ltd
12 Hill Rise, Richmond, Surrey TW10 6UA

British Library Cataloguing in Publication Data
A catalogue record for this book is available from the British Library

ISBN 0 85660 299 X

Typeset by Trotman and Company, Richmond
Printed and bound in Great Britain by Creative Print & Design (Wales) Ltd

Contents

After finishing university, you should be smart enough to spot a good deal when you see one.

As a graduate, we can offer you a first class package including:

- Special offers on graduate overdrafts and loans.
- Primeline, our 24 hour person-to-person telephone banking service.
- Commission-free travellers cheques and currency.
- And many other benefits.

If you'd like more details, simply call us on the number below.

0800 200 400

Monday-Friday 8am-8pm, Saturday 9am-6pm
www.natwest.co.uk

♻ NatWest

More than just a bank

CHAPTER 1 Introduction

If you want to make progress in your career (and who doesn't?), you must learn the skill of jobhunting, which bears little relationship to functional skills learned at school, college or in employment. Successful jobhunting is two parts dependent on self-marketing and one part on background and experience. Good interview skills will often win out over other attributes when it comes to landing a new job and this book tells you about the most successful strategies.

There is no such thing as a 'job for life' or even a job for everyone who wants one. Technology has opened and closed many doors in the past two decades, so that fewer people are required to produce more goods and services. For as far ahead as we can see the 'normal' level of unemployment in the developed world will remain higher than would have been regarded as acceptable only a few years ago and many jobhunters will have fallen off their career ladder midway as companies reduce the numbers once thought essential to the organisation. The 'middle manager' has become an endangered species and the highly qualified newcomer has to start at a lower level than before.

The successful careerist learns to develop core skills within a job and, more importantly, build up those which are transferable into other avenues later. That person could work in a wide variety of dissimilar fields provided that he or she recognises that skills are applicable across the board, for instance management abilities are important everywhere, although they may need modification to suit different industries.

Competition for a job begins when the applicant first contacts the prospective employer. This initial approach must be 100% right if it is to stand out from scores of other applications – there will be no second chance. Employers must want to meet the person behind the written words or there will be no interview – and that means no job. The most brilliant and charming people will remain on the sidelines unless they can win an interview when their personality and skills will be seen by the prospective employer, so the application has to hit the target and receive the vital invitation. There is no guaranteed way to win an interview but there are simple mistakes to avoid if you are to jump the first hurdle.

Successful jobhunting requires commitment and hard work – luck is no substitute for effort and self-motivation. The approach in this book will improve your chances of winning an interview and that is usually the only route to a job.

Whatever the unemployment figure and the changing nature of organisations, there are scores of people moving on every day, leaving vacancies to be filled by the right candidates. Your task is to make sure that you become the successful applicant by demonstrating that you can communicate your value to the potential employer via a good application and a convincing performance at interview. Never forget that jobs are not won by the best qualified people but by those who *appear* best qualified.

Winning an interview

CHAPTER 2

Marketing yourself

Are you one of as many as 95% of jobhunters failing to present yourself attractively in the job marketplace? Is your first step to produce a curriculum vitae (CV) or career history in the form of a list of schools, colleges, employers and dates with (perhaps) job titles added for good measure? If your CV also runs to many pages it presents a dreary and uninviting chore for the employer to wade through.

If you were selling a house or a car, you wouldn't list all the previous owners and dates of ownership, but would probably spend some time and effort on brightening up the item and marketing it to catch a purchaser's eye by emphasising its attractive features. If that makes sense when selling something valuable, surely it makes even more sense to do the same when trying to promote a career worth perhaps half a million pounds over a lifetime? Jobhunters, like house sellers, have to invest time, effort and money in their task to sell themselves to the right employer.

First steps

Good planning with lots of spade work is the basis of winning an interview followed by a job offer. Attention to detail now will save problems later. Most essential is a positive attitude – if you apply for a post thinking that you have no chance, your defeatism is sure to show. Optimism can easily give way to pessimism when months pass and success remains elusive, but pessimism can often be banished by a complete change of approach. And if your jobhunting efforts have slowed down recently, the ideas in this book will provide the change of direction that could bring success.

Setting your sights

Knowing your strengths and weaknesses will help you to answer questions at an interview in a way that brings out the best in you. Serious jobhunters will have clear career objectives about why they want to move, how they see their career developing and how a particular move fits into that pattern. You need to be able to convey positive reasons for your application at interview.

It is therefore a good strategy to make a list of reasons for changing jobs. It should include at least 20 entries, among which might be:

new location	better working conditions
more involvement with people	more money
greater security	new career field
more travel	less travel
greater status	more challenge
more teamwork	more independence
regular hours	more flexible hours
preference for bigger firm	preference for smaller firm
family needs	skills now redundant
contracting industry	promotion prospects
skills not fully utilised	new skills open up new prospects
more responsibility for people	reduced supervisory load
increased involvement in budgets	freedom from financial decisions

Consider your priorities and focus on what really matters so that future plans can be centred on these. Only then can you consider the type of work and industry you really want and which will satisfy your identified ambitions.

Skill and experience must be acknowledged but should not prevent a full self-examination which might point out the need for some retraining to achieve the desired change of direction. New skills can be acquired in many ways.

- Have you investigated the evening classes at your local college?

- Is there an organisation that might take you on as a voluntary worker for a few hours a week?
- Are there any interest or activity groups you could join?
- Can you extend your sporting prowess or hobbies, say in coaching or demonstrating?

Graduates will usually have made their choice before they embarked on their course, so how do they improve their chances? Often they have no work experience to offer except possibly vacation jobs – but there is no job or leisure activity that cannot provide experience. Higher education is for more than studying!

But whether or not you are a student or someone who is already part of the working world, there is a need to consider what skills can be offered over and above your job experience. You may not recognise some of the skills you can use to gain an interview, but now is the time to put that right by trawling through the past few years, examining every little example and thinking how it can be used to best effect.

The successful jobhunters are those who:
- are aware of the changing needs of companies and can promote the bits of background which are most relevant to the prospective employer
- know their strengths and weaknesses
- can sell themselves and open up possibilities where none seem to exist
- can work out where they stand and where they want to be
- can adapt to new circumstances
- have the self-confidence to carry it through with an action plan that will produce a winning application.

Others will fall by the wayside.

Unemployed?

The reasons for wanting to change jobs apply equally to someone who is unemployed, but they face an extra question – whether to stick out for career progress or take anything simply to get back into harness. The arguments for taking *any* job are strong: work brings in money above benefit levels, restores morale and avoids the 'unemployed' label on the next application form. However, taking a stopgap job makes it harder to find time to write your action plan and attend interviews, and future employers might just criticise you for losing your place on the ladder. One answer can be to sign up with an agency that supplies temporary staff for limited hours each week, but check with the DSS to make sure that your benefits are not adversely affected.

For the older person whose job was made redundant, taking a step down is often not a matter of choice but of necessity. Many doors are closed to the over-50s, despite the obvious wealth of experience they can offer; but some companies (eg B&Q) and charities positively welcome this generation, and who knows where the simplest opportunity might lead?

Turn your age into a plus point – for you and the company. Think about new colleagues, new town, new interests. Promote yourself positively: your stable outlook when the young are flapping or job-hopping can be just the thing a firm wants.

CV design is discussed later (see pages 11–14) but older applicants should opt for a Functional style, emphasising problems solved with the clear message that what you have done before you can do again. If you have a choice, apply by letter to help blur the age question by concentrating on years of valuable experience. Stress your drive and energy and limit previous experience to no more than, say, ten years.

Your date of birth is certain to be asked for on an application form. Never try to lose a few years – false information in an application can lead to instant dismissal. Instead, use your age to sell attributes and relevant skills you have gained over the years that could be capitalised on by the new firm. Provide useful and interesting information that will leap out at the reader – age then becomes relatively unimportant. Your aim is to win an interview. When one is offered you will have the chance to show how you could fill the post. For the moment, there is a preliminary hurdle to jump.

At the opposite end of the scale is the younger applicant, where the challenge is to convey maturity and experience when both are thin on the ground. Concentrate on previous achievements and responsibilities gained at work, college and in sports or social clubs. Tell your prospective employer about extra skills so that he or she relates your abilities as, say, a club secretary to the vacancy. Include any significant milestones or unique successes, such as if you passed your driving test the day after your seventeenth birthday or gained a GCSE in Japanese aged ten – they all help to flesh out experience.

For someone returning to work after a few years' gap, perhaps spent raising a family or as a carer, reflect the positive points from that period – you may not have been gainfully employed but you were certainly employed! Perhaps you once organised a toddler group, or worked from home, or became involved in a voluntary enterprise, or took over the household budget. However mundane it seems to you, it is worth examining it as an outsider would and seeing if it either added to your skills or could be related to the working world. If so, put it in front of a prospective employer as an extra asset that could contribute to the company.

Personal databank

One of the most important tasks in a jobhunting exercise is to prepare a personal databank. It can be very wearing to dig out a lot of personal information for each application, so it pays to gather it at the start and add items when something different is asked for by another potential employer. Most data is obvious and to hand, but some companies will want more detail – Civil Service applicants can expect to be asked for extensive personal information.

The databank also gives applicants the chance to spot their plus points as well as the minuses, which will assist in presenting information in a way that is most likely to win the interview. This will be a revealing task. You have a wealth of material and should use it properly – if you don't, nobody else can. Until you have put together your databank, you cannot prepare a decent CV or complete an application form.

What goes into the databank? The suggestions on the following pages are the bare minimum, so leave plenty of space for additions.

PERSONAL DATABANK

General information

Name _____

Address _____

Telephone: Home _____ Work _____

Date of birth _____ Age last birthday _____

Place of birth _____ Nationality _____

Height _____ Weight _____

Marital status _____ Children (No. and ages) _____

Passport No and expiry date _____

National Insurance No _____

Date driving test passed _____

Categories of vehicles covered _____

Education and training

Schools attended from age 11

_____

_____

Certificates gained with dates, subjects and grades

_____

_____

College/university attended with dates

_____

_____

Qualifications/degree with dates _____

_____

Subjects _____

Languages (state written, spoken, reading standard) _____

_____

Postgraduate courses_____

Clubs/societies joined at school and college _____

Offices held _____

Holiday jobs _____

Professional qualifications and dates_____

_____

Further training courses with dates, length of course and subjects

_____

Military service

Branch of service _____   Rank on discharge _____

Date entered _____   Date left _____

Service training _____

Interests and activities
List membership of clubs, societies, sports interests, hobbies, offices held
etc

_____

_____

Employment
Current/most recent salary _____ Salary objective _____

Immediate job requirements
List five jobs you could fill in order of personal preference

1 _____
2 _____
3 _____
4 _____
5 _____

List (from the above) the two jobs for which you are best qualified

1 _____
2 _____

State the job title you plan to have in

1. Five years' time _____
2. Ten years' time _____

Current/most recent job
Date joined/date left _____

Company _____

Business/product _____

Annual turnover _____

Job title(s) _____

Reporting to _____

Number reporting to you _____

Starting/finishing salary _____

Bonuses, allowances, awards etc _____

Reason for leaving _____

Description of job and responsibilities (note equipment under your control, proportion of total staff under your supervision, etc) _____

_____

Major accomplishments _____

_____

List reports or recommendations you made and what happened to them (include technical and administrative suggestions) _____

_____

List any major management decisions you took or recommended _____

_____

State what promotions you gained in this company _____

_____

List any other significant achievement or event when with this company

_____

Previous posts
Repeat the above data in précis for each of your previous three posts

Core skills
Against each core skill, list what you can offer which would most interest a new employer, including proof or evidence of the skill:

Communications _____

Teamwork _____

Numeric ability_____

Self-analysis _____

Problem-solving ability _____

Information technology ability_____

Other relevant information _____

_____

e, however, some dos and don'ts which you might consider before
ciding on your own preferred style and content.

The sole purpose at this stage is to create a desire by the recruit-
g company to meet you. Think of your CV as the dust jacket of a
ok – if it does not tempt the reader to pick it up, it has failed.

Your CV must be interesting and able to sell you to more than one
rson within the prospective company. Exactly what goes in or stays
it depends on space and the actual requirements for the job in
hich you are interested. Remember that whatever you include on
ur CV, it is your personal advertisement.

The presentation of your CV is of the utmost importance. It must
 clear, concise, well presented (ie not crammed, and with good
argins to ensure easy readability), accurately targeted and free of
ammatical and spelling errors or it will be on its way to the bin
fore it touches the recruiter's desk. It is also worth remembering
at if you do win an interview, the recruiter will turn to your CV
me and time again to refresh his or her memory about you, so make
re that you can talk intelligently about all the information you
clude in your CV, and can back up any claims with proof.

Choice of style

ow you present yourself is critical. Choice of style depends on the
pe of job you seek, together with your background and experience.
here are three basic styles, each of which has many variations:

1. **Obituary.** As dead as it sounds, this CV usually consists of a
   chronological list of schools and colleges attended with dates,
   qualifications gained, company names, job titles and duties.

2. **Historical.** This style offers education information and job
   details – the latter going back no more than about ten years, with
   earlier experience summarised. This approach, if well produced,
   is good for careers that show unbroken progress.

3. **Functional.** This kind of CV groups experience by functions
   such as production, personnel, supervision, etc. It is particularly

If you are a student you will have empty space where '[...] recent job' is to be entered, but you should use vacatio[n...] the gaps – whether working with the Post Office at [...] evening barwork – as it illustrates an ability to organise [...] mic and personal life as well as your reliability. Sandwic[h...] dents will have periods of industrial and college time t[o...] and should be able to elaborate effectively on their re[...] within their host company. Make the most of them!

If you currently have no vacation work or social activi[...] of, do your utmost to get involved in something that [...] strate you are not a couch potato! Mention, too, your inv[...] student societies or other activities as these can be indica[...] core skills. The point about including your interests and [...] is that they give an early indication to the interviewer [...] awareness, confidence, and willingness to relate to others [...] operate independently. These are attributes that a [...] employer will want to follow up on.

CVs that get interviews

The quality of the CV you send out will determine wh[en...] you are invited for an interview. It must be special to ge[t...] ten seconds attention before it is put on the 'reject' pile. [...] producing a CV that will get you an interview is, in time[s...] are hard to find, the most important single stage in jobh[unt...]

The chances of success in gaining an interview are per[...] 40, as ten people at most will probably be interviewed ou[t...] as 400 applications. So at interview the chances rise to a[...] ten. These statistics should focus your mind on the big iss[ue...] an interview invitation. They must always be remembere[d...] are tempted to dash off a 'standard' CV rather than thi[nk...] what the advertiser really wants from the applicant.

Making the right impression

There is no single CV format which will be right for all [...] or all recruiters and the final choice is very much up to [...]

useful where there have been many job changes, but requires very careful thought where work experience is limited. It is the ideal way to present transferable skills that, gained in one type of company, can be utilised in a new firm where the technology is entirely different. In carefully selected situations it will suit the student who wants to promote skills gained in, for example, student societies or vacation work.

Try preparing your CV in the different formats to see the advantages and disadvantages of each style to your own circumstances. You will probably quickly discard the Obituary style because of its dullness and failure to focus on achievements that you can offer the employer. It is also the style which perhaps 90% of other applicants will use and so, by choosing an alternative, you will stand a better chance of standing out and therefore winning an invitation to interview.

The winning CV

The material must be well written and stress achievements rather than merely list duties. The Historical and Functional styles of CV are intended to pick out the highlights of previous experience rather than give equal prominence to the less successful periods, which happens with an Obituary style CV.

Consider someone who has travelled the world for a few years doing nothing in particular. The Obituary style CV will suggest a drifter with no roots or career plan, unlikely to stick in a job for more than a few weeks before moving on again – hardly a good bet. However, a better style can present the same person as someone accepting challenge after challenge and broadening his or her experience, particularly by both developing and selling many skills in different countries, in order to achieve a special set of skills (and adaptability) at the end of it all. The difference is one of presentation – in the first approach, job interviews would not result; but in the second, most employers would be fascinated enough to offer an interview to see if such a dynamic applicant was worth bringing into the team.

Employers want to see what you could do for them, not your routine duties over the past decade. State your achievements in terms of increased sales, profits or cost savings; the interviewer can then see how they could apply to his or her firm.

The use of concise sentences and dynamic, positive words can add to the verifiable facts of your qualifications. Phrases should be carefully constructed to convey strengths, honesty and energy. Stick to the truth and do not exaggerate, as you will be expected to discuss and enlarge upon what you write when you are interviewed.

An open, natural tone is better than impersonal, third-person language. Words like 'established', 'planned', 'managed' make more impact than long woolly phrases. Avoid pompous or long-winded expressions – replace 'at that moment in time' with 'then'; 'as a result of' should become 'because'; 'in the event of' means 'if' and so on. Anyone can make spelling mistakes, but not in a CV. The recruiting employer is bound to think avoidable slips are indicative of sloppy work elsewhere.

The key idea for a student to put across is maturity – youth can be a plus; immaturity is definitely a minus.

A covering letter must stress things like:

- interest in a particular industry or profession
- drive and enthusiasm
- ability to learn quickly
- problem-solving talents
- physical energy.

The danger area for students is writing an entire essay when they are invited to give 'further information'. Recruiters are far too busy to take an interest in minor details and you need to be concise, always relating your words to the job and the firm.

For example, 'I play regularly for my college tennis/hockey/football/squash team and am social secretary of the Explorers' Club, responsible for organising social events and field trips for up to 30 people involving liaison with hotels and other clubs.'

This spells out the fact that the writer is someone with leadership qualities, can be a team member and has organising ability. Vacation or part-time work should be mentioned, stressing any extra responsibilities you have had and, of course, anything relating to the kind of job you seek must be covered. Seize the chance to make your application different and relevant rather than just one in a nondescript collection but avoid waffle to fill space. Think carefully about what you can say about yourself that will be of specific interest to the employer.

Using your CV

Now here's important advice: NEVER send a standard CV in response to an advertisement, even when one is requested. Nor should a standard CV accompany a speculative letter.

Consider the employers. They have vacancies to fill and will be deluged with CVs. Some of them will be inappropriate to the job, and some will be too sparse or wordy, forcing the recruiters to search for the relevant bits and wonder if they contain any information at all about what the candidate might do for them.

Conversely, picking up the successful jobhunter's CV, which will be tailor-made for the advertised post, with relevant skills and experience already highlighted, the employer will respond favourably to a candidate that closely fits his or her needs.

The message is clear. Using your personal databank and chosen style, prepare a CV angled to suit the job advertised or the company to which you are sending a speculative enquiry. Augment the sections most relevant to the job or where you are stressing your transferable skills and cut back on the other parts. Your positive response rate will increase measurably – always assuming that your experience comes close to meeting the needs of the job.

Never, under any circumstances, start a speculative letter with anything along the lines of 'I am writing to enquire if you have any vacancies…' This constitutes junk mail and spells 'time-waster' – it will be on its way to the bin before you can say 'jobhunter'.

It is best to keep general CVs for recruitment agencies to be considered against the wide range of vacancies they handle for a multitude of companies. Of course, this restricted use of a general CV means more work for you, but it will be fruitful work, especially if it encourages you to apply only for those jobs where there is a fair match of skills and needs.

CHECKpoints

○ Make sure your reasons for seeking a new job are clear in your mind.
○ Remember that any job you take can affect future moves and long-term career objectives.
○ Compile a personal databank to have information to hand when preparing CVs and application forms.
○ Be aware of both your strengths and weaknesses, and all the skills you have gained in work and through leisure activities.
○ Always tailor your CV to highlight the aptitudes and experience you can bring to each particular job vacancy.

Finding the jobs

Having produced a fully stocked personal databank and a CV you can tailor as needed, the next stage is to find potential employers and jobs. There are many sources, and to give yourself the best chance of winning an interview it is important to approach them in a way which makes you stand out from the competition.

Advertised vacancies

Approximately 60% of jobs are filled through advertisements. The major national newspapers publish a full range of 'situations vacant' and specialist posts appear in other newspapers and trade journals.

Don't overlook regional newspapers and magazines, as their lower circulation reduces the competition for applicants. And if you want to work in a particular region, get the local paper, such as the *Eastern Daily Press* for East Anglia or the *Glasgow Herald*. You can arrange for copies to be sent to you by the newspaper if you are outside its circulation area.

Many publications are available only to people and companies active in a particular field. It should be possible for a friend in that trade or profession to let you have a copy of the job advertisements from the publication – the contact might even lead to something more direct within that firm. If you get a copy of the whole publication, always read it through; it could contain informative articles to help you demonstrate recent knowledge of the industry at interview.

Advertisements appear in many journals and trade magazines and no jobhunter can buy them all. Many are available in public libraries, so visit yours at least twice a week. Find out what it takes and, if there is a title missing that would be useful, ask the librarian if it can be obtained for you.

A weekly publication, *Executive Post*, carries job advertisement aimed at qualified people and is available to read at Jobcentres and local libraries. The jobs will be of interest to all age groups in many different fields, but not all companies will use this publication to fill their vacancies, so keep looking elsewhere!

Responding to advertisements

When you see an advertisement that looks interesting, read it once quickly. Read it again and underline the main requirements for the job, relating them to your own abilities and experience. Ignore the fact that this might be a new field for you and think about what you do now that you could do for this firm. Ask yourself, 'Do I want the job?' and then 'Can I do it?' If both answers are positive, then apply.

Respond as required in the advertisement – by phoning for details, sending a customised CV or writing a letter etc – get that wrong and you are in the bin already as someone who can't read and can't follow instructions. Keep a copy of the advertisement and make a note of the name and date of the publication in which it appeared.

It can be worth applying even if you do not exactly match the specification. Clearly, if the advertisement stresses 'youth culture' or states that 35 is the top of the age bracket, it is not worth the stamp if you are over 50. However, if you do not possess exactly the right degree but have comparable qualifications plus relevant experience, it is time to think how you can sell the skills you do have to win your invitation to an interview.

If you telephone the company, ask to speak to whoever is doing the recruiting to 'obtain further details of the post'. This is worthwhile whatever way the advertisement required you to reply. You might not speak to the recruiter, but you could have a chance to speak to someone who has their ear and that is a useful start. Have a list of points ready to ask about; never give the merest hint that you fall short of the firm's requirements. Ask for an application form if one is indicated in the job advert, and/or a copy of the job description if available and politely close the conversation with a 'Thank you for your help'.

By now you are one step ahead of the competition – your name, voice and interest are known and you have shown initiative. Don't be put off if your telephone contact does not succeed – you may have caught someone at a very busy time or on a bad day. If you have responded quickly and politely without wasting their time or being difficult to get off the phone, you will have lost nothing and may have gained a lot.

Write to the advertiser along the lines of: 'Further to our conversation on (date), I confirm that I can match the requirements for the position of…,' and then briefly show how you do so, citing experience and qualifications that prove your skills and how they can benefit the employer. Keep this letter short and to the point – more than one page isn't going to be read.

If you are returning an application form or sending a CV, again include a covering letter which draws attention to those attributes that are important in the post. Your CV should also be angled towards that particular job.

Wise jobhunters will staple all their material together – CV, application forms and covering letters – as paper clips slip off too easily.

If you have received no response after two weeks, telephone and reaffirm your interest in the job as discussed on the phone and since confirmed in writing, giving the dates of both contacts. Say that you realise that mail can go astray, ask if your letter has been received and enquire whether your application is being considered.

Personal contacts

Many jobs are filled through personal contacts – don't let the apparent stigma of nepotism or old-boy networks deter you. Networking is now considered an important skill in the business world, and there is nothing wrong with using contacts to get yourself the right job. From the employer's point of view, there is always the risk of choosing the wrong person, however they are introduced, but if you have the skills they seek and are recommended by a good employee, they are more likely to invite you to interview, which is where you can prove your ability to do the job.

If you cannot meet the employer's needs, you won't get the job, but you have lost nothing and gained interview experience and knowledge of companies in your field. There might be a more suitable vacancy in the future that the company would discuss with you.

Your personal contacts might include former employers, business contacts, suppliers, bank manager, professional institute, colleagues, social club contacts, solicitors, MPs, councillors, friends, neighbours and relatives. Of course there may be many unsuitable suggestions, but don't ignore them all as they may point to a new line of thought. Don't, however, pin all your hopes on your personal contacts.

Social and public organisations

Active involvement in your trade association or union, chamber of commerce, professional institute, sports or social club etc, will bring you into regular contact with people who carry authority. If the choice lies between watching television or attending a local talk, dust off the good suit and go. Who knows who you might meet?

If you are already a leading light in your favourite organisation, why not think of organising an event that gives you a bit of personal publicity at the same time? Increased involvement in local affairs can only help – the more you are seen around, the more your name will be known. (Bear in mind that politics can open many doors, but political interest should never be mentioned to an employer at interview. Exceptions are obviously where the job is related to politics or you know the employer's views, but tread carefully in any case.)

Trade shows

Trade shows are useful as they bring together under one roof a large number of people from all levels in a particular industry. Staff from major firms will be around and, even if you only talk to a junior person, the information you can glean, including the names of senior people, could be valuable. And do not dismiss the idea of a visit to the hotel bars where exhibitors will be staying – an 'accidental' meeting in that environment can open a door. Remember that all you want is an excuse to introduce yourself, in person or by letter, to someone senior within the company. An easy line of approach is to comment on a new idea or product they were exhibiting and link it to your own interest or experience in that sort of development – you can follow this up with a question about job opportunities in their company.

For a student or someone keen to get into a particular field for the first time, trade shows are an unrivalled chance to see what is happening. The industry will be selling itself to the outside world and, although it will be presenting a rosy picture, its current state and its future will be there for you to examine. You can ask questions without making yourself look silly and you can collect handfuls of brochures – all useful pre-interview material.

Remember, too, even if you don't make a contact at trade shows, any interviews you later gain in that industry will benefit from your up-to-date knowledge. Just saying you frequently attend relevant shows will indicate to an employer your genuine interest.

Cues from the news

All the media regularly report news about organisations, new products, take-overs, mergers, expansion plans and so on. These can suggest useful openings to pursue. Find out who to write to (via a simple phone call to the company's switchboard) and, taking your cue from the report, in a brief letter to this person point out how your experience fits into the planned development of the new product or expansion programme.

There are distinct advantages to the news story approach. You will probably be the only person to have written and the company may really need help. If your letter reaches the right person, there are all the signs of a good match between someone (you) who seizes an opening when it appears and a boss who encourages such initiative.

Jobcentres

Jobcentres help to find new jobs for people who are usually (but not necessarily) unemployed. They are not compulsory and are free of charge to the user. If you have been unemployed for three months, Jobsearch Plus offers courses which, over three days, will help you to think through your possible range of jobs as well as assist in producing a CV, writing letters and dealing with application forms.

Someone who has been out of work for more than six months and signing on as unemployed, is invited to attend a Job Club, where additional support is available. No qualifications are required and so the mix of skills will vary considerably. Because of constantly changing rules, enquiries need to be made regularly with your local Jobcentre about the latest exemption categories and services.

Job Clubs will train people to write a CV and apply for jobs – including advice on being interviewed, so it is a worthwhile service. However, there are many different ways to win an interview, and because Job Clubs are used by so many people it is desirable to find an alternative approach that stands out from the crowd, as this book recommends.

Agencies, consultancies and registers

There are many reputable agencies and consultancies handling vacancies for companies. They either send replies straight to the firm or screen the applicants before producing a shortlist. A useful list of consultants and their specialisations is the CEPEC *Recruitment Guide*, available in libraries.

It is best to treat agency advertisements as if the advertiser was the actual recruiter. Telephone calls can often be disappointing as the consultant may know little about the post, but there are enough exceptions to make it a practical first step. A preliminary chat can create a good impression at an early stage and reveal useful information about the prospective employer.

You will be expected to have at least one interview with an agency, whether it is an initial meeting to get your name on the agency's database, or in response to a job advert. At these interviews, remember that the agency is looking for specific skills that they can match to employers' requirements – they are not careers advisers who will spend hours delving for your aptitudes, interests and personality in order to hand you the perfect job. Always prepare as you would for an employer, both in dress and positive attitude – you are selling yourself to an agent who will sell you on to an employer, with a mark-up, and you want to be sold to the highest bidder.

Agencies will require you to complete their own application forms. These often seem poorly designed, with minimum space for presenting achievements positively and they can be the equivalent of an Obituary style CV of dates and employers. From the agency's point of view, this makes for easy comparison of candidates in a process of rejection rather than selection; if you don't fit the employer's criteria exactly, they unlikely to put you forward.

If your background is unsuited to appointments being handled at the time your application is received, the chances of your being recalled a few months later are not too good. Computerised retrieval systems are usually efficient but names are deleted after a certain time on the assumption that the person will have found employment. It makes sense to contact agencies regularly to stay on their active list.

Agencies earn fees from the client company or the jobhunter, so their first duty is to whoever is paying the bill. Firms that charge the jobhunter offer varying services including career counselling, CV design and even marketing you. They should be searching their lists to find you a niche but you must be clear from the outset exactly what you are paying for and how long the service will continue.

Box numbers

Unless you want to swell Post Office coffers, forget box numbers. Your chances of getting a reply are remote and you might reply to the wrong person – even your current employer! The competition may be reduced because most people will not respond to a box number, but my advice remains the same – save your stamp.

Timing it right

Timing can be important when replying to an advertisement. If your letter arrives on the first day after publication, it will be one of only about 2% of the total received. The second day will see the arrival of about 20% of the responses, and the third day will bring about 40%. The numbers will begin to fall off after this and, by the end of the week, about 90% of the replies will have been received.

The first replies will be eagerly scanned by the firm, keen to see what level of interest the advertisement has attracted, but they soon get bored with tedious quantities of unexceptional letters and CVs, so your quality application needs to avoid arriving at the peak of their boredom. Unless you can be certain that it will arrive on the first day, it is better to wait until the peak has passed. No company is going to fill the job in the first day or two and you have nothing to lose by holding your fire. But don't delay too long as this could be seen as showing only a casual interest in the position.

Direct approach

The advantage of the direct approach is that you can present an enterprising image and will almost certainly be the sole applicant. If you use this method you must write to the decision-maker by name. The direct approach can tap into openings which have yet to appear but has to be lucky enough to appear on the right desk at the right time. Senior managers are well aware of the high cost of recruitment and, if outstanding people appear out of nowhere and present their talents convincingly, jobs can arise overnight. The chances of that happening during a recession are not high as companies do not recruit when times are hard, so the jobhunter who relies on this approach faces a very low response rate – most letters will be ignored.

When writing a speculative letter, never include a CV, as you are effectively saying 'Here is my entire background. You do the work – read it and pick out the bits you fancy.' Students are the exception, as their CVs will be more general, referring to part-time work and social activities which are best presented in CV format. For others a personal letter is best, emphasising your past achievements and concentrating on the firm and how you can help it – the employer is not interested in anything else. Don't begin by saying you are jobhunting or it will be the first and last sentence that is read.

Telephone calls are not a good idea in a direct approach. They are unlikely to reach the right person and, even if they do get through, it is improbable that the recipient is sitting around with nothing to do, just waiting to discuss job opportunities with a complete stranger. More probably your call will be considered intrusive and inconvenient, be met with an immediate 'No' and a door is closed.

There are ways in which the response rate of the direct approach can be improved:

- Write to someone by name and mark the envelope 'Personal'.
- Limit your letter to one side of A4 paper.
- Stick to good quality white paper and matching envelopes.
- Keep your sentences short, clear and simple.
- Sign the letter with a blue pen with your full first name, initials and surname.
- Type your name below your signature, adding your title (Mr, Ms, Mrs, Dr etc) in brackets.
- Show that you have industry knowledge in your letter or, if applying outside your own field, how your discipline applies to that company.
- Target your letter – concentrate (briefly) on what you can do for that company.
- Don't mention money.
- Don't send out letters at holiday times.
- Post your letter so that it does not arrive on a Monday or Friday – days when people are off or have other things on their minds.

'Situations wanted' advertisements

Putting a 'situation wanted' advertisement in a newspaper may seem attractive, but consider what sort of employer is going to look for staff that way? The only likely replies are from agencies and CV writers wanting to sell you their services.

Advertising in trade or institute journals might have more chance of success, but take advice from the advertisement manager on layout and presentation. If you use this method you will probably have to take steps to prevent your present employer finding out, so use a box number or, even better, the name and address of a friend from outside the trade.

Self-advertising on local radio and television has had spectacular results for the few who have tried it as they usually win news coverage as well. If it has not been tried in your area it could be worth the effort, but don't expect miracles!

CHECKpoints

There are many ways to approach prospective employers to gain an interview. Use your imagination and remember:

○ Personal contacts, membership of societies and professional institutes can provide useful leads.
○ Trade shows are a good way to get information as well as giving you exposure within an industry.
○ Advertisements, the major source of jobs, appear not only in national, and regional newspapers – industry specific adverts will be in trade journal and magazines.
○ A good advertisement will indicate the main job requirements – think about how you can sell your skills and qualifications to suit the job.
○ Timing of a reply to an advertisement can affect your success – be first or last to get most attention.
○ Jobcentres and associated services provide information and support to the jobhunter.
○ Introduce yourself to agencies to get your name on their lists, even if they are not advertising a specific job.

CHAPTER 4
Filling in the forms

Employers like application forms. They collect the information in a consistent format, allowing easy comparison of candidates and ensuring that important questions are answered. From the jobhunter's point of view, application forms are a poisoned chalice. They take time to complete, always ask the questions you least want to answer and cause great frustration by giving little opportunity to sell achievements while losing no chance to pinpoint weaknesses. Unfortunately, there is no escape from them if you want to win an invitation to the interview, but there are ways of making the best of a bad job.

As with other applications a typed or word-processed response is best, although the size of some forms may make that impossible. Always photocopy the blank form to check out the space available for your answers. This maximises your opportunity to list all your qualities and looks better than trying unsuccessfully, to squeeze in details in ever smaller handwriting.

Here are some tips for handling application forms successfully.

- Read the form first, so you understand and follow all the instructions. If it asks for black ink and personal details in capitals, use black ink and capitals.
- Don't let a company drop an application form on you when you arrive for interview. Ask in advance if application forms are used and for one to be sent to you. If they refuse and say you will be expected to complete it on arrival, either take your databank with you or cancel your appointment, as it will be difficult to do yourself justice in the limited time available.
- When asked for your employment history use the space to spell out your achievements. If that means you have to

summarise earlier jobs, do it. Concentrate on promoting your strengths and using recent experience to back them up.

- Ignore questions about past salaries – anything earned more than five years ago is irrelevant and your current salary is confidential unless you choose to give it at interview. If the form asks what salary you want, either ignore the question or quote a bandwidth of around 20% encompassing the expected rate for the job.

- If you are asked for academic results, unless you are a recent student, avoid giving grades. If you didn't do too well, you don't want to be discarded at this stage by admitting to something which, in mid-career, is irrelevant.

- If you are asked about leisure activities, offer a range of social and practical interests.

- Don't write flowery rubbish if asked to state additional points in support of your application. Use the opportunity to build on your achievements, quoting proof of skills, such as figures for improved sales or efficiency savings, etc.

- If asked why you left a previous job, never indicate any disagreements – the safest answer is 'career advancement' or 'promotion'. If you are asked at interview to enlarge upon that, you should find a way to show that the move did benefit your career, even if it can only be said with hindsight!

- Answers to questions must reflect the information in the job advertisement. If in doubt, write and rewrite the answers until you get them right.

- If a question does not apply to you, write 'Not applicable,' as a blank suggests you overlooked it. Put a dash in questions about salary.

- Never return an application form without a covering letter, and don't fold it any more than when the form was sent to you. Multiple creases are not attractive and first impressions can contribute to whether or not you get an interview.

- Make a copy of the completed form so that you can refresh your memory about your answers before your interview.

Some advertisements will invite you to send full details and then, in return, you receive a massive application form to complete. It is disheartening and may be indicative of a company's culture. However, if you want the job badly enough, you have no choice but to grin and bear it.

[CHECK *points*

To make sure your application wins you an interview, rather than hits the bin, here's some advice:

○ Always read the form first and follow the instructions carefully.
○ Copy the blank form and practise on it so you don't squeeze too much information in tight spaces.
○ Type your answers if possible, or use very neat, even handwriting.
○ Ask for an application form in advance rather than be faced with one at interview.
○ Use every opportunity to stress achievements in your answers.
○ Mention both social and practical interests in response to questions on leisure pursuits.
○ Reflect the advertiser's requirements in your answers.
○ Keep a copy of the completed form to read again before going to interview.
○ Include a covering letter as another opportunity to highlight how your skills suit the job, and staple it to the application form.

5 Testing times

Like fashion, the selection of applicants for a job goes through phases and although the interview is necessarily a permanent fixture, some of the other vetting tools come and go. Many firms use tests of various sorts to predict a candidate's suitability for an appointment (although for some of the character and intelligence tests, there is a lack of evidence to show if the results are borne out in practice). Whether or not you approve of them, as a jobhunter you should prepare yourself to encounter different types of test somewhere along the line. On the assumption that forewarned is forearmed, this chapter looks at some of the most common that you are likely to face before, during or after the interview.

Handwriting tests

Some employers ask for application forms to be completed in the candidate's own hand. This is often just to check on neatness of presentation but, occasionally, the application form will be submitted to a graphologist who will interpret the handwriting and report on the writer's personality. There is widespread disagreement on the validity of the practice but there are a few points worth considering.

- Irregular word spacing might indicate untidiness and lack of organisation.
- Excessive flourishes with large, aggressive letters may be the hallmark of a show-off.
- Writing over a letter or word twice is said to suggest dishonesty.
- Writing which slopes to the left (by a right-handed person) is thought to be a sign of someone lacking emotion.
- A rounded style of writing can indicate immaturity.

However accurate these observations may be, because some firms trust them, they can affect the success of your application. You can't change your handwriting drastically over an entire form, but you can ensure any written material the company sees is neat and legible.

Psychometric tests

Psychometric tests should be completed with one thing in mind – always give truthful answers! The way a person performs in a job is not just a question of ability, their personality also plays a major part, so this sort of assessment provides useful extra information for the employer seeking a certain personality type.

Among the many characteristics a test might uncover are a person's tendency to worry in a range of situations, willingness to take risks, view of change, approach to others – whether outgoing or reserved.

The answer to any one question is unimportant but there could be up to 500 questions and inconsistency is certain to show through if you try to disguise your responses – and there are likely to be traps designed to pick this up. Even if you were able to keep up a particular pretence over the entire paper, your problem is not knowing what the company is seeking – do they want a modest, quiet person or a real up-and-at-'em individual?

A college careers office and your local library will have samples of psychometric and other tests for you to browse through. All job-hunters should be looking at test examples for a full idea of what they might face, but two simple examples are offered here.

Select the two most important reasons for working.
1. Chance to show initiative
2. Good working conditions
3. Good working companions
4. Good boss
5. Security
6. Money
7. Good hours
8. Interest in work
9. Promotion
10. Credit and recognition.

The desired answers are numbers 6 and 8, as the majority of people are assumed to need an income but prefer to enjoy the way in which they earn it. No one would suggest that the other points are unimportant, but the question is one of priorities.

An alternative type of question might try to discover how you see yourself, as in the following example.

Indicate the words which most and least describe you:
Persuasive
Gentle
Humble
Original

This test was used for a management position to find people who saw themselves as 'persuasive' and rejected the description of 'humble'. Someone may like to be thought of as 'gentle' rather than 'persuasive' but they are unlikely to commend themselves to a potential employer if they mark anything other than the preferred answers.

Most questions will be much more subtle than these, as the intention is to find out about your real personality.

Aptitude tests

Aptitude tests can indicate a person's particular interest or skill, thus adding to the recruiter's knowledge of the applicant. Their real value lies in trying to avoid square pegs in round holes. Tests can be revealing – even the most brilliant mathematics graduate can score poorly in numerical reasoning tests, which would indicate to the employer that that person lacks practical skills.

They are almost always confined to people entering the working world for the first time. There will usually be a number of separate papers, looking at entirely different things; for example, checking spatial abilities, spelling, arithmetic, understanding of mechanical concepts, ability to work accurately and decision-making.

Clearly someone trying to enter the field of design needs to score well on spatial tests, but perhaps their spelling ability is of little importance. If that same individual was seeking work in the print industry, and liked the idea of copy checking, then spelling takes a higher priority over almost everything else. The test score is then compared with a 'norm' for people of a similar age and educational background so the results are comparative rather than absolute.

Books of aptitude tests are available in most libraries and bookshops and it is well worth your time and effort practising for what might lie ahead. The questions will not be the same, but knowing the approach can only help.

Someone who is in mid-career might find themselves taking an aptitude or skills test at the interview to prove their ability. Obvious examples are typing tests for keyboard-based jobs, proofreading in publishing and printing, or showing mechanical or technical skills, such as using specialist tools or equipment, or putting together the pieces of an electric device. If you think you may face such a practical test, don't panic and always relax when doing the exercise. If your skills are rusty, practise beforehand – you can't get better over-night, but you will be more confident about your own level of competence, and therefore more comfortable when doing the task.

Testing advice

The main advice is to relax, read or listen to the instructions carefully, then complete the paper or exercise as quickly and accurately as possible. A responsible interviewer will discuss the results with you, although you might have to wait until the interview for feedback.

What does the company get from tests with all the ifs and buts taken into account? Tests were once seen as the answer to most recruiting problems, but their ability to predict success, particularly at managerial level, is uncertain. They may elicit temperament and personality but a good interviewer will also be doing that and, faced with any conflicting evidence, is likely to back his or her own opinion. Psychometric tests are also time consuming so, until there is a greater degree of predictability, they will remain an option that only a relatively few firms will use, but for which jobhunters must be prepared.

Ask before your interview if there will be any tests. If the answer is positive, some background research is needed. Applicants generally dislike tests and, if asked, there is no reason why you should not say so – it can do no harm to have an alibi if you do not do well! Of course, you can decline to attend an interview if tests are used or, if no warning was given, you can choose to opt out, but it is unlikely that your application will get any further.

Many tests are not intended to be completed in the time allowed, although speed and accuracy clearly affect the score you achieve. Failure to finish does not automatically mean your application will founder, but if you have time to spare at the end of a test, always go back over any questions you were worried about earlier. Beware of guessing at answers where you are offered alternative solutions to problems. Some tests carry penalties for wrong answers and you should ask about that before you begin.

Above all, never underestimate tests. No company will offer a job to someone based on test results alone but, just as important, there will be a question mark about someone who does badly in them or shows inconsistency in their answers, no matter how impressive they were at interview. Tests, like application forms, are another method of weeding out candidates, not a method of selecting them.

CHECKpoints

- ○ Tests supplement interviews, not replace them.
- ○ Tests can be used to find out about aptitudes and personalities and to measure skills.
- ○ Books on certain types of test are available in bookshops and libraries – use them to familiarise yourself with the format.

6 Pre-interview issues

Winning an interview is harder than landing a job but, having won it, there is still work to be done to ensure that the outcome is an offer of employment. You must get it right if you want to be in control, whether or not you decide to take the job.

To get a job offer, you must research your prospective employer, learn how to control the interview and put your best foot forward.

Finding your way

An early task is finding out how to get to the interview – you may need a road map to work out your route or you may have to check train or bus times. In both cases you need to know how long the journey will take. Consider, too, where you will park (if you drive) or how long it will take you to get from a station or bus stop to the company's premises. You might even have to plan an overnight stay, but in that situation it is possible that the company will suggest a suitable hotel and arrange it for you.

These may seem like obvious administrative plans, but they will ensure that you arrive punctually, unflustered and totally focused on performing well.

Researching the company

More importantly, there is simply no excuse for not finding out as much as you can about the company where you have won your interview. Being asked 'What do you know about us?' and replying 'Not a lot' indicates that your interest in the company is insufficient for you to have investigated its background. It is essential to know about the company's products or services, its markets, how many people it employs and its recent financial results. By knowing that and relating it to the job you are seeking you can show how valuable you could be to the firm.

Where do you find the information? There are many sources, including:

- the company itself (annual reports, promotional material and graduate recruitment literature – often available in libraries or college careers services)
- libraries (including the City Business Library in London)
- Companies' House
- employees and company sales teams
- competitors and their sales teams
- suppliers
- creditors
- products
- The Daily Telegraph information services (available through libraries)
- trade or professional associations
- unions
- Department of Employment
- local chamber of commerce
- college careers offices.

Public libraries keep many directories with information about an organisation and your local librarian will be able to help you. If a firm is not well documented, ask the library to make enquiries for you at other branches, or ring the local college to see if they have anything. Graduates are fortunate in being able to find out about many companies through their careers offices.

What should you try to find out about a firm? It all depends on the job and its level, but could include:

- ownership, finance (profit/profitability, expansion plans, cash flow), return on capital invested (well capitalised or struggling, contracting or expanding, diversifying, inter-firm comparison, rationalisation, take-over attempts, share value and trend)
- personnel at director level

- opinions of people who know the firm well (knowledge of management and their lengths of service)
- past redundancies
- succession plans
- staff turnover record
- is the job a new one? If not, what happened to the previous incumbent? Why no internal promotion?
- company organisation structure
- products (range, profitability, market share, problems, research and development, competition, new products, exports, new markets, rationalisation of products)
- production (sources of raw materials, new or obsolete machinery, safety record, shift working, quality control, transport arrangements, retail or wholesale outlets)
- policy on public relations, advertising, marketing, personnel, finance, administration and so on.

Obviously it will be impossible (or unnecessary) to find answers to everything, but try to include areas outside of your immediate focus. Some information will be subjective, some of it more solid, but the more you know, the better impression you will make on the interviewer and the clearer you will be about whether or not you want to join the company.

Timing of the interview

Interviewers are only human and have their good and bad days, as well as peaks and troughs each day. Successful jobhunters need to avoid the problem days and times and, with forethought, that should be relatively easy.

Midweek is by far the best choice. Many people are not at their best on Mondays or Fridays so why take the risk? The best time is probably first thing in the morning, so that other interviewees are compared with you (the next best choice is the final interview of the day, so that you leave a lasting impression). However, if you are not a 'morning person', change the time of the interview. You won't know whether or not the interviewer is a morning person; you just have to take your chance. But do try to avoid the worst possible time, which is first thing after lunch – commonly known as the 'graveyard slot'.

If you want to change your appointment, telephone the firm, confirm your interest in the post and ask for an alternative appointment. Having won an interview, no reasonable company will refuse your request if you offer a credible reason why the time they suggest is inconvenient for you – make sure you have one. If you are offered a choice, accept the one that suits you best, without getting into lengthy negotiations.

If you are applying to an organisation that runs a panel interview system, you have no choice but to accept the date and time offered.

Looking good

Dressing for an interview can be a problem but very much depends on the type of employer you are considering. For jobs in the law, accounting and finance or industrial management, smart, conventional dress is a must. In other situations where creativity and individuality are rated highly, as in the media, the fashion world or advertising, conventional dress might count against you.

The most important thing is to look clean, well presented, and dressed in a way that will be acceptable to the prospective employer and appropriate to the work environment. You need to ensure that your appearance does you no damage before you have had a chance to show what you could do for the firm. A casual sweatshirt and jeans is not yet accepted interview dress, even though you may be wearing them once you get the job.

If you don't own anything suitable, now is the time to make one of your better wardrobe investments. You can always brighten it up or tone it down depending on the type of company you have applied to. For example, you might think white or blue shirts/blouses boring, but they are a safe bet, except perhaps in creative or youthful environments, where you might be expected to show more individuality.

Any hint of shabbiness – a worn shirt collar, missing buttons, laddered tights, damaged heels, unbrushed hair – will do nothing for the positive impression you are trying to create. Many interviewers look at a candidate's shoes to see if they were cleaned that morning – an obvious point for your attention, even if irrelevant to job ability.

It is best to avoid bow ties (which can be considered frivolous), dark glasses (they hide your eyes and, it might be thought, your intentions) or anything really over-the-top. Strong perfume or aftershave (or too much garlic the night before) can also be a put-off for your interviewer.

Appropriate appearance is important both for the experienced jobhunter and for students. The latter may see little reason to change from the relaxed codes they usually follow, often on a tight budget and supplemented by second-hand garments. But in order to make the best impression at interview, it is important to toe the conventional line as much as possible – save your fashion statements for when you've got the job.

Think about the impression you are giving. Doesn't a doctor in jeans and T-shirt seem less professional than one in a white coat? He or she may not be, but appearances matter a great deal, and clothes, personal grooming and attention to detail can help you look like a winner. Clothes will not get you a job, but they can lose you one.

Don't overdo it, however, and appear so immaculately and expensively put together that you intimidate the interviewer – moderation is the name of the game.

Then what about the second interview – should you change or wear the same again? There is very little chance the interviewer will remember what you wore before but there is something to be said for showing that you have more than one interview outfit. The way you dressed the first time clearly did not put off the interviewer so it is likely that the same general appearance will be right.

One final word about presenting yourself successfully. Try very hard, even if you are hopelessly hooked on tobacco, to avoid smoking for at least an hour before your interview. The smell lingers, and many people actively dislike it. The same goes for alcohol – however much you feel you may need Dutch courage. If your interviewer smokes or drinks, or invites you to do so, decline politely without indicating disapproval.

Be punctual

A company is entitled to think that a candidate who arrives late is generally unreliable. Being late for an interview could cost you a job. The solution is to arrive with time in hand to gather your thoughts. If you are delayed, telephone your interviewer's office as soon as possible to explain what has happened; the interviewer will appreciate having been warned and will probably await your arrival. When you arrive make an immediate apology for the delay and then forget about it. You might even win some sympathy for the problem that caused your lateness, and that will break the ice. You will also have succeeded in showing confidence in yourself and relieved the interviewer of the task of setting a flustered candidate at ease.

If you arrive early enough, a walk around the area might tell you something about the company and its environment.

- Is the site open and well laid out, or is it cramped, which might indicate poor working conditions?
- Do the buildings look well cared for or are they run down and held together with nails and bits of string?
- Are there any staff in sight? Do they seem over-worked, or are they idly twiddling their thumbs?
- Are there any derelict buildings on the site? If so, does that suggest the firm is contracting?
- Is there any sign of new building work in progress?

None of this evidence is conclusive, but it helps to build up a broad picture of the company you are visiting and the impression gained might sway your decision if you are offered a job.

Plan to arrive at the interviewer's office about five minutes before the appointed time. If you are any earlier, it can create some embarrassment and if you are any later, it gives you less time to unwind and can suggest that you cut things too finely.

Some interviewers will deliberately keep you waiting. If you are offered an apology and perhaps a cup of tea or coffee, accept gracefully. Look at any company catalogues or trade journals in the waiting area – you might learn something and will give the impression that you are keen to add to your knowledge.

If you are still waiting after half an hour, ask how much longer you can expect to wait. If the delay extends beyond that, the next step might be to ask if the interviewer would prefer you to make another appointment, as obviously this is a very busy time for him or her.

Should you leave without having seen the interviewer, write to the company on your return home and explain that it was impossible to wait longer as you had other arrangements or a last train to catch etc. Consider very carefully whether or not you want to get involved with the firm – there may be a message there for you.

CHECK*points*

- ○ Know exactly where the interview is and how to get there, so you can arrive focused and on time.
- ○ Research into a company is essential before attending an interview – prove you've done your homework.
- ○ All information gleaned, positive or negative, is useful in making a decision if you want to work at a company.
- ○ Try to make the interview appointment for a the time of day you are at your best.
- ○ Appearance matters – get it right for the job, and do yourself justice.
- ○ Never be late for an interview – or the first impression you will make is unreliability.

CHAPTER 7 Interview dos and don'ts

The preliminaries

Chapter 6 showed that, when you have won the invitation to an interview, there is more to do than accept and turn up without any other preparation. You should telephone to accept it (or change it as necessary), ask who you will be seeing and then confirm the arrangements in writing. You should also enquire about the time allocated for the meeting – is it to be one hour or half a day?

There are many types of interview and an employer will sometimes use more than one variant at different stages of the selection process. The most common is the one-to-one interview, usually conducted on the employer's premises, although sometimes held in a 'neutral' location such as an hotel room. Other interview formats are outlined in Chapter 9. In all cases, there are essential steps to be taken by the job applicant – just as you planned your jobhunting strategy, now you must consider and plan your interview behaviour, leaving nothing to chance.

You may be a bit nervous, and that is perfectly normal, but some people are among life's worriers and over-anxiety can ruin an application. Remember that an interview is an *exchange* of information to find out about mutual suitability – you're interviewing them too; so, if it helps, try to forget about *your* performance and concentrate on how the company performs in presenting itself to you. Also take elementary precautions by getting a good night's sleep before the interview. If a mild tranquilliser might help, there is no harm in taking one, but a stiff drink beforehand is never the answer.

If you have followed the advice given in this book, you will turn up at the interview neatly and appropriately dressed, on time and well prepared. You will have the added confidence that your preliminary contacts with the company have marked you out as noteworthy, and your interviewer will be keen to discover if you measure up to his or her expectations. Interview technique is vital, but it is your approach, rather than the fine details, that matter.

You may also learn that you will be having other than a one-to-one interview but that is no reason to panic. Whatever may be in store, there is still a need to come over as an intelligent, diplomatic and capable individual who is moderately outgoing without being overbearing.

Give the right impression from the start by greeting the interviewer, and any others present, with a friendly smile and firm handshake. Return your interviewer's greeting with your own 'Good morning/afternoon', and use his or her name. He or she will have used yours, and it is an early courtesy to get names right. If other people are introduced, your problems multiply, but try to use the names correctly – it helps to get you off to a good start. Most interviewers will next try to set the candidate at ease with some small talk but there might be a plus for you if you take the initiative and offer some remark about the weather or the state of the roads.

Interviews should be a two-way process, a discussion between equals, both giving and receiving information, and thus helping both sides to reach the right decision. Occasionally an interviewer will adopt a parent–child attitude or attempt to grill the interviewee. These approaches are best handled by the jobhunter taking control of the interview. This means remembering and using the principles of the Seven Point Plan to ensure that important matters are covered (see page 76).

Setting the scene

If you are wearing a coat and it was not taken from you before you were shown into the interviewer's office, ask where you might put it rather than risk throwing it on to someone's favourite chair. Before you sit down, angle your chair towards the interviewer, or lead interviewer, if more than one person is present. From time to time, you should acknowledge any other people in the room, even if they remain silent, by the occasional smile or answer in their direction.

Avoid carrying a large briefcase or any clutter – settle for a document case and/or handbag unless you need to take a portfolio of your work. If you have a mobile phone, ensure it is switched off and out of sight before you enter the firm's premises. There is nothing to be gained by arranging to receive an 'urgent' call in the middle of your interview, and everything to lose.

The main act

Every interview is different – different people, jobs and situations – and there is no one key to success, but there are some dos and don'ts. The interview is your chance to deploy your personal skills developed at college, at home and at work. You will be expected to demonstrate your ability to relate to people, to present yourself effectively and to negotiate issues that come up during the interview without becoming antagonistic under provocation or caving in to pressure. The following list is not exhaustive, and it is unlikely that any one candidate will have to handle more than a few of the points at a single interview. It mainly applies to the one-to-one situation, with minor modification to cover other circumstances.

✘ Don't use your interviewer's first name even if they use yours. But if you are invited to do so, use the name sparingly.

✘ Don't immediately take your jacket off even on the hottest day unless invited to do so. If the interviewer is casually dressed you might ask after a while if there is any objection to your taking it off.

✔ Do have some material in your document case even if it is just your research into the company and your list of questions – it will show that you have done your homework. Avoid carrying too much, as that could suggest you are disorganised.

✘ Don't put anything on the interviewer's desk – it is his or her personal space and may be jealously guarded. Even a coffee cup should be kept in your hand unless someone has put it on the desk for you or the interviewer has offered you a space.

✔ Do answer in positive terms – even about the weather. Positive answers are easier to understand and you will come across as optimistic rather than pessimistic.

✔ Do speak at a normal, controlled pace. Many people talk too quickly or mumble because of nerves, so be aware of the possibility and try to avoid it. Clarity of speech is vital in a job involving contact with the public and may be what the interviewer is looking for.

✔ Do slightly understate your desire for the job. Make the firm want you, but beware of playing hard-to-get too well. When the interviewer starts selling you the job, things are looking good!

✘ Don't put up with indignities. If your interviewer is rude, does that tell you anything about the firm and, if so, do you really want to work there? Remember, however, that rudeness could be deliberate and part of a stress interview technique (see Chapter 9).

✘ Don't forget the job requirements as set out in the advertisement, or any other information you have obtained, and tailor your replies to this end.

✔ Do try to project your sincerity, achievement and enthusiasm, and avoid becoming over-serious – the occasional light aside or smile as you answer a question can go a long way.

✘ Don't be caught out by the occasional, deliberate silence. If a gap does arise, ask one of your prepared questions – but choose carefully and relate it to the earlier conversation.

✔ Do ask a question to show that you have done your homework. If you are a student, you might ask how many former trainees are still with the company after two years. At a more senior level, you might comment on sales figures. In addition to showing interest and knowledge, you win a moment's respite from the interviewer's questions.

✔ Do make the occasional complimentary and knowledgeable remark about the firm or its goods or services – but don't overdo the flattery.

✔ Do listen to what you are being told – it is inexcusable to ask something that your interviewer told you two minutes earlier. Use the information when you come to write your follow-up letter.

✘ Don't answer an ambiguous question without asking for clarification. It will show commendable caution and save a wasted journey down a blind alley.

✘ Don't waffle. If you do not know the answer to a question, say so – talking nonsense is much more damaging.

✘ Don't behave like a politician by answering your own question rather than the one just put to you. If you cannot give a straight answer, say so and explain your point. For example, if you have been unemployed for some time and are asked why, don't spend the next five minutes talking about how the economy in your area has been hit by the downturn in the demand for widgets thanks to some Directive from Brussels, going on to discuss your view of Britain's further involvement in Europe. Simply explain that you have a clear ambition and, although you have had various stopgap jobs, you have had to make sacrifices in order to follow up suitable opportunities.

✘ Don't assume you are more knowledgeable or skilled than the person interviewing you. Interviewers are unlikely to hire someone who talks down to them, or who they perceive as an immediate threat to themselves.

✘ Don't put your needs above the firm's. A company wants you to demonstrate that you can match the job specification and can deliver the goods, and you do this by explaining how your skills in previous jobs or societies are easily transferable to the job under discussion.

✔ Do think about the structure of the interview. If you are being interviewed by a personnel professional, he or she will be following a framework, probably Alec Roger's Seven Point Plan, which is designed to ensure that the vital areas are covered. If this is not happening, you need to prevent the session from deteriorating into an aimless chat without it being apparent that you have taken control. (A summary of the Seven Point Plan is on page 76.)

✘ Don't play with your watch or jewellery, fiddle with your fingers or buttons, or engage in other distracting mannerisms.

✔ Do avoid controversial topics that polarise opinion – religion, politics and race are forbidden territory unless the appointment is in one of these fields. If you are asked about a difficult subject, the middle ground is safest until the conversation moves on.

✘ Don't name drop – the 'name' might be a personal friend of your interviewer, or they might have been cold shouldered by them.

✘ Don't let your interviewer bombard you with an avalanche of questions with no chance to answer before the next one is fired. If your interviewer tries that tactic, wait for a pause then say 'You have asked a number of questions, let me answer the first one'; after that, if you still hold the floor, ask for the next question to be repeated. Trying to answer ten questions in a row will mean that you talk for too long and go off the point – it is better to pass the responsibility back to the interviewer.

✘ Don't argue with your interviewer. It may be that he or she is playing devil's advocate to see how you react. If things get tricky, just listen carefully, and pick up on a point on which you agree, then develop it.

✔ Do answer a straight 'yes' or 'no' to questions where appropriate, but remember that detailed replies will usually be wanted. A good interviewer will ask 'open' questions that call for full answers, but if that is not happening, you must assist.

✘ Don't repeat the question in your answers. You could get away with it once or twice as a ploy for time to think, but it becomes irritating after that. Remember that body language can be as informative as what you say and your actions may show that you are playing for time.

✘ Don't try to answer a question before the interviewer has finished speaking. It is bad manners and suggests that you leap into action before you have all the facts.

✘ Don't let your answers ramble on for too long. If more detail is wanted, let the interviewer ask further questions in his or her own time.

✔ Do avoid like the plague statements such as 'I think', 'I believe', 'If my memory serves me right'. They add nothing and quickly irritate the listener. Try also to avoid clichés such as 'basically'; if you must use a similar adverb, try 'essentially', 'fundamentally' or 'primarily' if only for variety.

✘ Don't string everything together with 'and' or 'but'. Pause, take a breath, add a mental full stop then continue. Beware of the 'ums' and 'ers' that pollute speech. Avoid using 'You know', 'You see' or 'Right?' in every sentence. If you suspect that you have such habits, tape a mock interview with a friend and then listen to what you sound like.

✘ Don't lie at interview. However, no one is obliged to tell the whole truth. For instance, you might truthfully say, if asked, that a move to another part of the country would not cause your family any worries when the whole story might be that you have split with your partner and one of the reasons for wanting the job is the chance to start again elsewhere.

✘ Don't give away information about your present employer or it might be thought you would do the same again and that could cost you the job. If the pressure is piled on, beware of the company you are thinking of joining, as their interest in you might only last as long as they can pump you for useful information.

✔ Do make clear to your interviewer that you can adapt your core skills to the company's needs. Spell it out, for example, by explaining that you have been able to use your bookkeeping or managerial abilities to benefit a local committee.

CHECKpoints

Gaining an invitation to an interview is like winning the first game of a tennis match, not the set. To promote yourself successfully at interview remember the common-sense dos and dont's.

○ Be friendly and confident.
○ Never argue – politely but firmly change the subject if you are uncomfortable with the questions.
○ Try to avoid distracting mannerisms of speech and habit, such as fiddling with your clothing or hair.
○ Always relate your skills, experience and strengths to the job in question.

Asking and answering questions

Questions to ask

Candidates are always invited to put questions to their interviewers and failure to take up the offer will probably mean that you are branded as lacking imagination or initiative. Good questions do not arise out of thin air and the successful jobhunter will, before attending the interview, have prepared at least 20 points to raise. It is a good idea to take a written list with you, so that the interviewer can see that you have done your homework.

People often worry about what to ask at an interview, but it should be one of the easiest stages of all, especially if you have researched the company beforehand. Try to plan questions for everyone that you expect to see at the interview. Some points will have been covered during the natural exchange of information; it should not be a problem to develop some questions from there, but you can always fall back on stock questions to put at intervals or when invited to do so.

Finance and personnel

Asking the interviewer to outline the short- and long-term objectives of the company will prompt a pause for thought and give you a break. Enquiring about the major problems expected in the job will provide points to raise at a later stage. You may learn about new products, competitors, expansion, new machinery, new staff and so on. Questions about the organisation structure in a larger firm, or about where the job appears on the organisation chart, are good for showing that you are alert and interested in how the business functions.

If your interviewer offers financial information that is more recent than any you could find, ask how the next quarter's results are expected to go. Ask how the company prepares its departmental budgets and if you would be involved. Ask what freedom of action you would have when it comes to spending the money.

Ask what happened to the person whose departure has created the vacancy and how long he or she had the job. If they only survived a few months, make light of the point and ask about the predecessor. Try to find out how long your interviewer has been with the firm. The answer will help you to judge any attitudes expressed and how they conform to the company's official line. It is probably unwise to ask that question directly, but there are bound to be chances of gently leading the interviewer into confiding the information if you think it would be useful to you.

If there has been a discussion on recruitment, ask about future expansion plans. Ask about training programmes for yourself and people at other levels within the company.

Jobhunters who have researched the company thoroughly will have no difficulty in coming up with points to raise. However, if the interviewer provides a wealth of detail as part of his or her introduction and information exchange with you, you can always fall back on why, what, how, who, where and when if you want a respite. These are guaranteed to get the interviewer talking, but remember to listen to the replies.

Naturally you will want to know about salary, benefits, holidays, etc. You may already know some of the answers from the advertisement or have been given the information by the interviewer but, if not, it is better to leave these matters until the end of a second interview. To ask sooner could suggest you are overly concerned about the rewards and less keen on the responsibilities which the job carries.

Training

One vital question (of importance to students especially) is the company's training system, how it is planned and whether those who complete it find development and promotion within the company. You need to find out if the firm has a structured training programme or proactive training policies.

In good firms, proper training programmes have clear objectives, but students ought to make sure about training arrangements before they find themselves wasting time with a second-rate introduction to the working world.

Questions to anticipate

Every interviewer will ask about your duties and responsibilities in your current or previous post or, if you are a student, about any activity in which you have been involved, and all jobhunters must be ready for such obvious questions. There will, of course, be plenty of non-obvious questions. For instance an interviewer might ask what football team you support and why or what's your favourite soup. The intention is to see how a candidate reacts when caught off guard, and their ability to take the unexpected in their stride can be important.

There will be many questions asked, and it is unforgivable to win an interview and throw away the chance of a job offer through failure to prepare for the obvious. You don't want to learn any responses parrot fashion but, particularly if you have weaknesses in your background, you need to consider beforehand how you would answer questions like the following.

- What are your short- and long-term career ambitions?
- What is your management style?
- What would be your ideal job?
- What are you looking for in a job?
- What criticisms are made of you in your present job?
- Why do you want to move?
- How long do you expect to stay with us?
- How long before you expect to show results in this post?
- What is special about you that makes you our ideal choice?
- What salary are you expecting?
- What is wrong with your present company?
- How do you rate your present company?
- How do you define success?
- What is your health record?
- Can you stand pressure? Give an example.
- What is your greatest failing?
- What is your strongest attribute?

- How have you changed the nature of your present job?
- Why haven't you found a job so far?
- Why aren't you earning more at your age?
- Why did you only get a second-class degree?
- Why did you go to college instead of getting a job and studying in the evenings?
- What do you think graduates have to offer this firm?
- Aren't graduates an expensive luxury for a firm?
- Do you think graduates are better than those without any qualifications?
- What are your five greatest achievements so far?
- Do you prefer line or service management posts?
- What are your objectives in your present job?
- What do you think of your boss?
- What does your boss think of you?
- What interests you most/least about our job vacancy?
- What do you like/dislike most about your present job?
- Has college been worthwhile or a waste of time?
- Describe yourself in three minutes.
- Are you creative? Give an example.
- Are you analytical? Give an example.
- Are you a good manager? Give an example.
- Have you increased sales/productivity?
- Why do you want to leave your present firm?
- Have you reduced costs?
- Have you hired staff? What do you look for?
- Have you fired staff? How did you handle it?
- Are you a good leader? Give an example.
- What do your staff think of you?
- Why do you want to work for us?
- If you could work for any company in the UK, which would it be? Why?
- What other jobs do you have in the pipeline?
- Why do you think you have management potential?
- How much do you know about us?
- How do your colleagues see you?

- Do you ever lose your temper? In what circumstances?
- Where will you be in five and ten years' time?
- What books/magazines/newspapers do you read?
- What are your leisure activities?
- Are you a good team player?
- Are you a loner?
- What questions would you ask if you were in my chair?

The serious jobhunter will carefully consider their answers to the above questions and many others which these will prompt. You can expect questions that are aimed at finding out both personal and professional attitudes, aptitudes, as well as weaknesses.

Be prepared to demonstrate skills and strengths with examples of your own experience, and to face questions designed to startle you into an immediate personal response. You can't anticipate every question but, having thought through the points, it will be easier to respond coherently when the questions are put. Note carefully what kind of person or company you are dealing with and, in the same way that you tailored your application or CV, tailor your replies.

A word about sex

The question of sex discrimination remains unresolved, and women can often feel that they are not yet being given a fair deal. The fact that women will still be asked about family responsibilities and men will seldom face the same questions is discrimination, but it happens. It is unrealistic to pretend that firms do not worry about investing training in a young woman instead of an equally qualified man on the off chance she may leave within a short time, or will prioritise her family over and above the employer.

A female jobhunter might also expect some testing questions about her attitudes to hypothetical situations, such as discrimination in the workplace. The legality may be doubtful, but it is best to anticipate and be prepared to be asked about things such as your views on what constitutes harassment, or your family responsibilities or your partner's prospects – and politely but firmly deflect the personal questions you are not comfortable with. As with any apparent rudeness or insensitivity in an interview, you will give a more positive and confident impression if you don't respond heatedly.

Interviews held for internal moves can be tricky, as the interviewer may have heard personal details on the grapevine – that you're trying to start a family, that your partner has just left you and you need to increase your salary, that a relative is seriously ill – and want to question you about it. This again is more likely to happen to female applicants, and however near the legal mark, be ready to steer the discussion back to your application and ability to do the job.

Demonstrating ability

For people seeking jobs as technicians, toolmakers, designers and other practical work, the evidence of their employability is their work and the reputation of their present and previous employers. It is relatively easy to judge skill and capabilities when they are physical and measurable. In the case of a management position the skills are harder to define and even harder to prove.

Self-projection

An interview will reveal many of the attitudes and views that make up the personality of the candidate. You have to project yourself in positive ways by thinking about the questions you are asked and answering clearly, selling yourself in an honest and attractive manner.

Much of the question-and-answer process is a psychological battle and how you answer a question can be critical. For example, it is essential to have an acceptable reason for wanting to leave your present job, and probably the one before it, but there is nothing wrong with admitting a mistake when you joined the wrong firm before that. Naturally you were too young to spot the danger signs but now, looking back, you can see what ought to have been obvious then!

Certainly you have no criticism of your present employer – but see a possible response to this question below. If you have been made redundant, remember it was the job, not the person, that became redundant – you don't have to treat it as a failure. And, as a student, you are determined to find the right job, not just any job as you have a career in mind.

You will nearly always be asked to state your greatest strengths and weaknesses. You need to have an answer ready – to decline to answer is modesty taken too far. There will be many areas in which you are strong so prepare a suitable, honest and positive reply. On the other hand, it would be arrogant to claim no weaknesses, so the skill is to answer light-heartedly, then offer a point which many people might see not as a weakness but a virtue. For example, admitting to irritation with untidiness might even gain you some plus marks.

Other answers might be along the following lines.

'How long do you expect to stay with us?'
'I'm looking for a career opportunity and, as long as you are happy with my work, I will stay while I can advance my career. I hope that will be for a considerable length of time.'

'How long before you would expect to show results in this post?'
'I hope I will be contributing in a very short time, but it will take time to find out how things work in the company. Once I know my way around I believe my experience will quickly become useful and results will follow.'

'What do you think of your boss?'
'My boss is a first-class person and I have learned a lot from him/her. I have really enjoyed working with him/her and the rest of my colleagues.'

'Why do you want to leave your present firm?'
'I'm keen to find additional responsibility and earn more money. I want to add to my experience and, because I see no openings in my present firm in the foreseeable future, I have to look elsewhere.'

'Where do you see yourself in five or ten years' time?'
'That depends on the job I accept and the company I join. I am not

concerned about job titles but more interested in finding an enjoyable and rewarding position. My five and ten year plans will depend on the responsibilities I am given.'

'What are your leisure activities?'
'I have a wide range of interests, though the demands of work and family mean that there is a limit to the time I can give them. I particularly enjoy doing practical things and have built a playhouse in the garden for the children. I am also a member of a local club and that involves many different people and activities.'

'Are you a good team player or a loner?'
'My record shows that I have achieved results in previous jobs that depended on teamwork and my ability to motivate staff. I recognise that someone who runs a department has to take decisions alone, based on the best information available. I have no problems in doing that and I know that decisions have to be properly communicated to all concerned. In my student days I was elected to one of our union committees where teamwork was essential to get results.'

'What questions would you ask if you were in my chair?'
'Well, it has been a very interesting meeting and I think everything has been covered. However, if I was on your side of the desk, I would ask the candidate if he (or she) was still interested in the post...'

CHECKpoints

○ Prepare a range of questions to ask using your research of the company and knowledge of the industry.
○ Ask about training opportunities, especially if you are a student.
○ Avoid asking about benefits such as holiday allowance until second interview.
○ Work through answers to likely questions, especially those about your strengths and weaknesses.
○ Be prepared for personal questions, and always respond firmly and politely.

CHAPTER 9

Other selection methods

The informal chat

What happens if there is no particular job under discussion but you have been invited to 'come in and chat things over'? In that situation, the interviewer might open the conversation by asking you to 'tell me about yourself'. Avoid the temptation to launch into a half-hour monologue. Start your reply 'I am interested in the company because...' and then take a maximum of two minutes (time yourself at home) to explain how your experience could be useful to the firm, opening up various avenues for your interviewer to explore with your encouragement.

Another opening approach is to say 'I am looking forward to learning a bit more about the organisation' and go on to sell yourself in about two minutes. In both cases, you will want to guide the conversation along your chosen path, but make sure you get around to asking 'As you have no specific opening at present, what area could your company see me fitting into?'

The informal chat can be a total waste of time if it has no structure as, at the end of it, no one has any real idea of what has been achieved or what might happen next. The candidate must avoid that by deciding in advance how he or she wants things to go, then making it happen.

Stress interview

This is not unlike a courtroom cross-examination and is used to make the interviewee say something that might otherwise be held back. It is characterised by frequent interruptions, critical comments on answers, repeated questions on specific points, extended silences and a generally hostile attitude. There may be a good reason – for the company – why such interviews are conducted, but they can be difficult to get through if you're not expecting them.

There are only two ways to react: either tell your interviewer that you had not expected the Spanish Inquisition or stay cool and answer calmly without arguing. The choice depends on your temperament and need for the job.

Trial by telephone

In these days of costly travel and expensive overnight accommodation some, applicants find themselves being interviewed by telephone as the firm (or more likely a recruitment agency) responds to a written application by phoning the jobhunter.

Phones ring at the most inopportune moment and suddenly, from being relaxed, the receiver of the call can find him or herself deep in discussion over a much-wanted job. It can be a difficult situation to handle and, if mistakes are made, it can mean losing any further chance to win the job. What needs to be done to save the situation?

The way you answer the phone is of crucial importance – think of your own reaction if, when you call someone, you get a gruff 'Ullo?' It does nothing to build confidence. Now that we are advised not to answer our home telephone with the number, an acceptable alternative is needed. 'Hello, the Smith household' is one solution.

Parents need to teach young children to answer the phone and immediately ask who is calling. Avoid even this, however, when you are expecting an important business call.

Sometimes an appointment will have been made for you to receive the call. You should therefore be fully prepared to take the call in a quiet room. Your jobs file, including the advertisement, must be at hand to refresh your memory, as asking the caller to remind you of the details suggests that you have no serious interest in the post. You should also be able quickly to find your own application, which would have emphasised your plus points. Just as in a face-to-face interview, you are trying to sell yourself, and a stumble now is just as damaging as in any other situation. You need to be in control of the situation and ready to have a focused conversation with the caller that will lead to the next stage.

However, if the call has come at an unexpected or impossible time – the cat might be having kittens or you may be saying goodbye to visitors – explain the situation briefly and ask if you could ring the caller back at an agreed time. Most people will accept that it is likely to be much more fruitful if the candidate is prepared for the call rather than trying to wing it.

If the caller ends with thanks for your time but regrets that you are not quite the person required for the post, your telephone technique may need attention.

Most people find it harder to achieve a rapport on the phone than face to face. It requires greater concentration as you are relying on just one of your senses instead of all of them and your body language can play little part. You can of course smile and sound enthusiastic and positive during the conversation. Sit comfortably and don't smoke, eat or drink when on the phone.

If you can sell yourself on the phone simply by having thought about it in advance, you will have thinned out the field as few of your competitors will have done so. But you will not get the job on the strength of the phone call alone – it is just like an application form and is another way of deselecting people. The real test is the personal interview which should follow, and that is what will bring the job offer.

Panel interview

Panel interviews are common in public appointments such as teaching and local government, where everyone wants to be in on the act and no one appears to have absolute authority for selection. They have obvious limitations but persist despite these.

In a panel interview the candidate is usually seated in front of a row of up to 12 people. Each will have questions to put. Most will repeat points already answered, and seldom will there be any effort made to build on a question or its answer. It is almost impossible to present yourself effectively in this situation as there will be limited time available for you to talk. You don't want to deprive someone of their question with the possible result that you might also lose their vote when it comes to the panel making its decision.

All candidates (perhaps 12 or more) attend on the same day and at the same time. Everyone usually waits together in one room and each is called to interview in turn. After the briefest of interviews – probably no more than 20 minutes – the applicant will be returned to the waiting room until all have been seen. After the final interview there could be a long wait while the panel deliberates; the successful candidate is then called into the room and offered the job. An immediate assent is usually required as the panel will want to offer the job to their second choice if the preferred applicant declines.

One panel member will then be despatched to tell the unsuccessful applicants that the appointment has been offered and accepted.

There is often the feeling at panel interviews, particularly if an internal candidate gets the job, he or she had already been chosen but the process had to be completed to give an impression of fairness. The best a serious jobhunter can do is try to control events and answer in a way that brings out achievements and abilities. Responses should be directed to the person asking the question, but remember to glance at others from time to time. Questions may be invited from the interviewee but anything more than the most basic will probably be met with something about 'dealing with that later if you are successful…'

When you return to the waiting room, do not discuss your experience with the other candidates. And beware of any comments they might make, as there could be an attempt to mislead you.

Group interviews

Group interviews are often used to select a number of candidates for similar jobs (often school-leavers or graduates) where the focus can be on personality, as there is no job experience to call on and the company wants to see how people react in the situation.

The group interview will usually be followed by a one-to-one interview for the chosen few. In the first stage everyone will be assembled in one room with a number of observers who will note how applicants handle a set of situations. The group might be invited to discuss a current topic or invited to suggest one itself. The observers watch developments, noting how everyone contributes to the discussion.

- Do they try to dominate?
- Do they bring others into the debate?
- Do they knock down someone else's opinions?
- Do they build on another person's ideas?
- Do they keep the group on the point?
- Do they introduce red herrings?
- Do they summarise what has been said before moving things on further?

If the group has to nominate its own chairman, it would be unwise to volunteer unless you have experience as, without it, you will soon be sidelined when the group finds out that you cannot control the members. That will then mean that you are neither chairing the discussion nor able to contribute with the same freedom as the others. You thus become a loser twice over. However, if you can do the job, and you do it well, you will have earned some merit marks.

If you are not the chairman, you must contribute to the discussion. You should offer balanced comments, putting the pros and cons of the case before giving your view. You must be seen to listen carefully to others but don't, under any circumstances, try and shout someone down or attempt cheap debating points – you are not in the House of Commons! There is nothing wrong with a light-hearted comment, but not at someone else's expense, rather let the group have a smile at your skill in defusing an awkward moment. And when you do make a point, do so succinctly.

If a meal is included in the event, be aware that social conversation with your fellow interviewees will be noted by the firm's staff. Behave as naturally as you can during the meal and in the group discussion but, especially if you are normally quiet, realise that you must make an effort or you will not be noticed. A few pertinent contributions will cause you to be seen as someone whose views are considered and valuable compared to those determined to take centre stage.

Anyone for tennis?

Interviewers will sometimes involve candidates in gimmicks. Someone applying for a job in sales might be invited to sell the interviewer a glass of water as the solution to all medical problems. Another possibility is being asked to make a mock phone call and to describe a pattern of shapes to the person at the other end, the idea being to see if the applicant can put words together coherently and intelligibly – not an unreasonable requirement for a post in which communication is important.

It is difficult to prepare for such events, and the response will depend on the background of the jobhunter. Someone with sales experience should not find the exercise too difficult, but a newcomer to the job market will not be as fluent. However, the interviewer will be taking past experience into account and marks will be won simply for effort and a willingness to knuckle down and get on with the task. Again, remember that a bit of humour can go a long way.

Skills tests

Selling a glass of water may be a skills test for a sales rep but other jobhunters might find themselves tested in other ways. For example, someone whose job will involve much written work should not be surprised if their spelling is checked. That can mean being presented with a list of 100 words, some of which are correctly spelled and some with common errors, for the applicant to sort out. Numeracy is also important and may be tested with mathematical exercises.

There are tests for almost any aptitude (see Chapter 5 for a discussion of these), and usually younger applicants face these as, without a lengthy job history, they may be the only indicator of ability. Where you need to show what you can do, for instance if you are a designer or photographer, take a portfolio of suitable examples with you.

Money matters

If your interview has gone well, salary will almost certainly be mentioned towards the end of the first meeting or, if not, at the second interview. It is probably best to fend off any detailed discussions on the topic until other things have been covered but, at some stage, serious negotiation will have to take place.

An advertisement may have indicated a salary range, or you might have gleaned the information during the interview without it being specifically raised. Most companies have a figure in mind for a post, even if they advertise the salary as 'negotiable', and they are unlikely to move far from their original idea. However, for anyone who has been headhunted there may be a chance to agree something a bit over the odds. For students stepping on to the first rung of the ladder there is little scope for negotiation – the company will have a figure firmly fixed and is unlikely to change it.

Negotiating salary is an important part of the interview process and will be considered in greater detail in Chapter 10. Be aware that it will probably be mentioned at some point in all types of interview, so you should have some idea of your requirements.

References

It is generally safest to withhold the names of your referees until you are offered the job; you must be certain that there will be no contact with your current employer without your explicit consent. Note, however, that the normal practice in jobs such as teaching is to request references at the first stage.

The referees will know you as employer, client, college tutor or friend. Students can offer the names of employers where they have done vacation work or part-time weekend jobs, and using an academic referee (such as a tutor) is acceptable. You must always ask your referees in advance and tell them about the type of job involved so that they can tailor their replies to highlight your suitable qualities for the position. Warn them if they might be telephoned instead of receiving the more usual written request. Have a variety of people to ask and select them carefully each time.

CHAPTER 10

The last rites

Talking money

Few interviews are likely to omit the question of salary and, towards the end of the meeting, serious negotiation may take place. If a job carries a salary range of £15,000–£20,000, the firm will be trying to fill the job at close to the lower figure but, in practice, will probably go up to about mid-point of the range. An applicant could therefore expect a maximum of about £17,500. Paying a newcomer any more may leave the company worrying about the effect on existing staff, so there is no point asking for it.

If your present salary is relatively low, include in discussions any allowances you enjoy to indicate your full remuneration package and thus your full worth. Resist exaggerating, however, as this is easily discovered if the firm checks with your old employers or your tax records will give the game away. Students have little room for manoeuvre, as the company is likely to have rigid entry points, although smaller firms might have more flexibility.

If you are unemployed there is pressure to accept almost any salary, and you have to decide whether to take this chance and get back on the ladder or to wait for the next interview. Everyone has their own commitments and must calculate carefully, as there can be no single answer to the problem.

Changing jobs for career advancement should mean a salary increase of around 15–20% at least. The cost of relocating may be partly reimbursed but there are scores of hidden extra costs that cannot be recovered and an insufficient salary increase will soon disappear. Consider carefully matters such as the cost of new school uniforms, subscriptions to new leisure facilities or college courses, as well as the obvious household expenses.

Before negotiating terms you need to know if the job is yours, but a straight question on that point is likely to bring a reply along the lines of 'We have still to make our decision, but just supposing you were offered the job, what salary are you expecting?' It is a tricky question, but you can say something like 'Assuming I am offered the job and decide to take it, I would expect the complete package is worth about £X', where £X is just above the mid-point of the advertised range or is a fair figure in the current jobmarket.

If you have been offered the job and accepted it, further discussions on salary should follow. It would be a mistake to leave it for the firm to write to you with an offer, as you either accept it or say 'No, unless…'. That could bring a 'Take it or leave it' response so, before the final interview ends, you should at least try to negotiate a likely salary range if not the final figure.

If you are the only person who can do the job, or have been headhunted, you are in a strong position. It is more likely, however, that there will be someone in the wings who is just as capable of doing the job and who will do so for less money.

In any negotiation it is best to let the other side see how you are thinking rather than just produce numbers out of thin air. Your future employers will acknowledge that yours is a good case and it will help them to meet your goals. It is usually better to talk of a percentage increase over your last salary, as the figures sound lower than if you talk in thousands of pounds.

If an offer is made at interview, indicate interest and ask for time to consider it, pointing out that you have others (family, etc) to involve in the decision. If the firm really wants you, and has made a definite offer, it is not going to withdraw it because of your request. But do not use this as an excuse to come back and ask for some further improvement – that is disingenuous and could result in the offer being withdrawn.

If the salary offer falls short of your hopes, discussion might turn to future prospects. A promise of a review in three or six months instead of a year could be a solution. Better help with removal costs might also be a way of improving your benefits; others include life assurance, private medical care, company car and petrol, share purchase scheme, discounts on company goods and profit-sharing schemes. And if you have to find temporary accommodation while selling up and moving, will the company help out over a reasonable period? Taxation might affect some parts of the package and this also needs to be considered.

When the final deal is struck you should show your delight with the prospect of the new challenge, the firm and the future, and give your new employers every reason to feel that they have gained a valuable new member of the team.

A successful jobhunter will also be a successful negotiator neither being ready to concede defeat nor trying to inflict it on others. If things are sensitively handled, the final offer can be a handsome advance on the initial one without making your new firm think they have paid over the odds and, perhaps, already beginning to wonder if they have done the right thing.

Closing techniques

If the interview has gone on long enough for you to have sold yourself to the best of your ability, you might need to help the interviewer to end it. He or she may have covered the ground, answered your questions and be shuffling papers. Take the hint. Don't ask any more questions unless there is something vital to be resolved, but gather together whatever you brought with you or have been given.

You have reached an important stage. You want to know how the interview has gone, and it is also your last chance to clear up any misunderstandings. Look at your interviewer and say something like, 'I have enjoyed discussing this job and how I might fit into the company. However, if you feel there are any gaps, can you please tell me about them so that I can try to answer the points.' Most interviewers will mention something, and you should respond by thanking them and briefly reselling your relevant qualities. Don't strain the interviewer's patience – or time – by pushing for further points.

You will want to know where you stand, but resist asking outright 'Have I got the job?' – it is far too blunt and, especially if your performance was borderline, could count against you. Take a softer line with 'I appreciate that you will have other people to see, but I would welcome any pointers that you can give me on the strength of my application.'

Interviewers will often try to side-step this question by saying that they have other people to see and therefore cannot answer. All you can do is to smile and press the point by reminding the recruiter that you are asking for comments on your application. Tread carefully, though, as you do not want to damage your chances, but merely let your interviewer know that you interested in the job and simply want to hear what those chances are.

It is probable that your interviewer will have decided whether or not to shortlist you towards the end of the interview, but if there is genuine uncertainty, there is no reason why he or she should not say so. Unfortunately, some interviewers will reply 'No problems' when what they really mean is 'No offer', which limits your chance of clearing up any points of confusion, or getting feedback on your performance.

Of course, if the interviewer says 'You've got the job', show pleasure, but take care – you need the offer in writing. Say something like 'I am delighted and look forward to receiving your formal offer. Have you a starting date in mind?' In that way, you have indicated your intentions but you are not fully committed to accepting the job until you have it in writing.

Now is the time to depart. If you do not know the result of the interview, thank the interviewer for seeing you, ask when you can expect to hear a decision, shake hands firmly, smile and say a simple 'goodbye'. Then go. Save any curses or punching the air until you are well out of sight! Then forget the job until you have an offer and concentrate on the next interview you have lined up.

Learn to control, allow for chemistry

Over the span of their careers, serious jobhunters will become accomplished at the interview game, learning to tailor their presentation to suit the circumstances. The pace of a discussion can be an indicator of how things are going. Sometimes it will become clear during an interview that this is not the job for you – but that is no reason to give up. Perhaps your skills could be used elsewhere in the organisation? Maybe creating the right impression on this occasion will lead to a future, more interesting vacancy?

Sadly, some interviewers are not up to the job. Many will be personnel staff who have little excuse, but a common difficulty arises when the interviewer will be the candidate's boss. Interviewing will not be his or her usual area of expertise and the jobhunter must make allowances. A good interviewee will quickly spot the problem and help the discussion along, ensuring that the Seven Point Plan is followed (see page 76) and thus gain the unspoken but grateful thanks of the interviewer. Adept, but tactfully discreet, controlling of the situation could help you win the job.

It is tempting to judge a company by its interviewer, which may be justified when you are subjected to a stress interview. However, jobhunters can only use what they see and know of the company in order to decide if they want to join it, and one individual should not unduly colour a decision over and above all the other evidence.

Employers interview because they need to recruit staff, and they use the best technique they know – even if they make mistakes or their methods are not always appropriate to the position on offer. They certainly do not want to lose a good applicant by appearing incompetent. Give the company the benefit of the doubt for any mistake the interviewer makes. Most will play it straight; the exception usually stands out like a sore thumb.

No matter how good an interviewee you become, you will not win a job offer every time. You will lose some because you spoke too little or too much; too loudly or too quietly. Your interviewer may have taken an instant dislike to you. You may have asked for too much money. You may have the wrong accent. You may have slipped up on one vital question. The 'chemistry' may have been wrong. Don't despair – you can't win them all. But you can learn not to make avoidable mistakes and promote yourself positively and effectively at interview.

CHAPTER 11 After the interview

After an interview most people consider that all they have to do is await the result. Wrong! Yes, you have worked hard, perhaps travelled many miles, and have undergone considerable mental strain over a concentrated period. You will not have been the only good candidate and the others will have had similar experience to offer the employer.

If you want the job, the obvious course of action is to do something to remind the firm that you were different and their best choice. How can you achieve that? There are two things you can do – phone or write. Choose the latter and send the letter within 48 hours of the interview. Sell yourself for the last time to this company by writing more than just 'Thank you for seeing me'. Use the opportunity to refer to information that was given to you, showing that you understood it and have thought about it. Your letter must indicate your continuing interest in the job as the company might be hesitating between you and someone else and this could make the difference. A letter will not change the decision of an employer who has made up his or her mind either way but, in marginal cases, it might just tip the balance.

Letters that are unanswered after ten days or so can be followed by a phone call. You only need to ask when you can expect to hear a decision – maybe the firm's letter has gone astray? Your persistence can do no harm and might even improve your chance of success as it is possible that a final decision has not yet been made. Your continuing interest can only be seen as positive and convince the firm that yours is the name waiting to be written into their plans.

If your application fails, don't be tempted to dispose of all the material relating to the post – you will then have nothing on file if another vacancy appears with the same organisation in the future. Do you really want to have to research it all over again? It is more sensible to retain the name of the firm, the person you saw, the job in question and the dates. Better still, keep copies of all the relevant correspondence and try to analyse why your application failed, as that could help your presentation to this or any other firm in the future.

Accept or decline?

Do not hand in your notice to your present firm until the written offer from your new employer arrives. When it does, only you and your family can make the decision – accept or decline? By now you will know as much as you are likely to learn about your prospective employer, you will have details of the full remuneration package and an idea about your new boss. If you are uncertain, take 24 hours to think the decision through – you can always blame a postal delay if the firm rings and asks for a decision. But if you have any doubts, what are they, and should you take the risk? Doubts today could mean serious misgivings tomorrow.

If you decide to turn down the offer, write to the company and thank it for its interest but explain that you have had another offer that more closely meets your career plans. Never be anything other than polite, as you could find yourself applying to the same firm sometime in the future for another post.

If the offer is one you really want, it matches your needs, and you and your family are in agreement about that, telephone to accept it, telling the company that you will send written confirmation immediately. Take great care not to leave any ambiguity in your letter – you must not let your acceptance seem to depend on the company's readiness to let you have a green car rather than a red one (or some equally trivial issue).

It is important to accept an employment offer by telephone and written confirmation. A phone call is essential because your letter could go astray and the firm conclude that no reply means no interest and so withdraw the offer.

Your acceptance letter should include a sentence saying how much you look forward to taking up your new responsibilities, and giving the date you will join the company. You should also mention the main points in the company's offer letter – items such as salary, length of notice, holidays – along with other important matters that were discussed or are part of a service contract.

That leaves the task of writing your letter of resignation to your present employer, giving proper notice. As when you accept a new job, resignations should be given verbally and confirmed in writing. Your objective should always be to part company with your present employer on the best possible terms. You want them to think well of you, especially if you might need references.

The final step is to update your personal databank – then it is all eyes to the future in the new post.

A final word

Finding a job is hard work. Finding the right job is even harder. It requires creativity, patience and resilience, and it can be hard to focus all these essential qualities if the job market is dull and you are currently on the sidelines. Persistent individuals succeed even in hard times. You will need the support of those around you so be careful in moments of exasperation.

The successful hunt for a new job begins with thorough preparation before you even apply. There is no point in telling yourself that you can do the homework the day before the interview – if you take that approach you will not present yourself as well as your competitors.

Every post has to be filled. Make sure *you* fill it by promoting yourself at interview in the most attractive way. Can any sensible employer then reject you?

For anyone who values their career, the investment of time and money in their own future will make the most of their own and their family's lives. It is a very demanding and exciting task in which the rewards, when they come, match the effort. Using the techniques described in this book, you can avoid the obvious pitfalls and turn positives to negatives.

■ You will not be overlooked for an interview for presenting yourself poorly to the company in your CV or application form.

- You will have created a good impression by arriving at interview on time, calm, appropriately dressed and showing confidence in yourself.
- You will not lose out because your record is weak, poorly explained and you failed to think it through in advance.
- You will reinforce the positive impression you make by showing you are interested in the company and have researched it properly.
- You will not find yourself in the 'Thank you but no thank you' pile because you omitted to build on your strengths and so encourage the firm to want you on board.
- If you are a student, you will have proved that your academic qualification is just one part of your value and that your extracurricular activities have helped develop a range of skills you can offer an employer.
- You will have proved your commitment, teamwork, versatility and enthusiasm through your involvement in various student societies, local groups or voluntary organisations.
- You will have matched your skills and strengths to the job in question and convinced the interviewer of your ability to do the job with flair and enthusiasm.

Good luck and happy jobhunting!

CHAPTER 13 Useful information

The following addresses and publications are believed correct at the time of writing but changes occur frequently and information should always be checked.

Addresses

City Business Library, 1 Brewers Hall Gardens, London EC2V 5BX Company information of all types.

Companies' House (for England and Wales), Crown Way, Maindy, Cardiff CF4 3UZ. Or Companies Registration Office (for Scotland), 102 George Street, Edinburgh EH2 3DJ. Records on 'Limited' companies.

Publications

CEPEC Recruitment Guide, published by CEPEC Ltd. Directory of recruitment agencies and search consultants.
Executive Grapevine, published by Executive Grapevine Ltd. Directory of executive recruitment consultants.
Getting into Job Opportunities, Kathleen Houston, published by Trotman. An introduction to successful jobhunting.
Guide to Working for Yourself, G Golzen, published by Kogan Page. Step-by-step guide to self-employment.
How to be Interviewed, D Mackenzie and P McDonnell, published by the British Institute of Management. A brief guide on interview technique.
How to Succeed at Assessment Centres, published by Trotman.
The Image Factor, Eleri Sampson, published by Kogan Page. A guide to effective self-presentation for career enhancement.
Jobs and Careers, published by Newsquest Ltd. Weekly publication with a full range of vacancies.

Job Hunters' Guide, published by Encliffe Ltd. Weekly publication with a full range of vacancies.

Kelly's, published by Reed Information Services. Information on 90,000 UK companies.

Know Your Own IQ, HJ Einseck, published by Penguin. A source of psychometric tests.

Kompass, published by Reed Information Services. Company information.

Major UK Companies, published by EXTEL. Financial information on companies in FTSE All Share Index.

Opportunities. Weekly newspaper for public sector vacancies. Available in libraries.

Selection and Assessment at Work, G Jessop and H Jessop, published by Methuen. Aptitude and psychology tests.

Seven Point Plan, Alec Roger, published by the National Institute of Industrial Psychology. A brief description of selection interviewing using the Seven Point Plan.

Who Owns Whom? published by Dunn & Bradstreet. Guide to company ownership.

Women's Rights: A Practical Guide, A Coote and T Gill, published by Penguin. A guide to the law concerning discrimination against women.

The Seven Point Plan

The Seven Point Plan is a recognised framework used by interviewers assessing job applicants. It was developed by Alec Roger and was first published in 1952. Although no plan can guarantee success in interviewing, its use ensures that the interview takes an organised look at the candidate. This is a brief summary of the points that are considered.

1. **Physical.** Does the candidate have the necessary physical attributes for the job? These might include height, weight, strength, vision, ability to withstand heat/cold working indoors or outdoors. Is the person's appearance satisfactory and his or her voice suitable for the job in question?
2. **Attainments.** What educational qualifications or work experience does the job holder have?
3. **General intelligence.** How much general intelligence does the job require? How quick on the uptake does the person have to be? Is the applicant over intelligent for the job, which may lead to dissatisfaction on both sides?
4. **Special aptitudes.** Does the job call for any special abilities such as being able to draw or write well? Is a talent in music or numeracy needed? Special aptitudes are particularly important when selecting someone who may not be highly intelligent but has a marked skill that can be harnessed in certain types of work.
5. **Interests.** Can the applicant demonstrate a particular interest that would be especially useful in the job? Is a practical, artistic, social or intellectual interest desirable in the successful applicant?
6. **Disposition.** Does the job require the person to be specially self-reliant, cheerful, strong willed, persuasive and so on?
7. **Circumstances.** Does the job call for any particular time or financial sacrifices? Does it require the person to be away from home a lot? Is his or her personal background likely to have a bearing on the ability of the candidate to do the job well?

The Seven Point Plan (of which there are variations) does not do anything by itself, but the overall outline remains as valid today as when it was first introduced. It is a way of classifying information, and there is no requirement to take the headings in any special order. It acts as a set of handrails, not handcuffs, for the interviewer. If you realise that it is being used, you know that you are being interviewed by someone who is trying to be professional, which must be a good sign.